koko &roo

A Book of Prayer for Children

Dedicated to the loves of my life, my precious family.
Giving God all the glory for this incredible opportunity.
May every child know God, His love for them,
and may He always be a guiding light to their feet.

Originally published in the United Kingdom.
Repton,
Derby,
DE65 6PZ
United Kingdom.

Written by © Melissa Madsen
Illustrated by Irina Akimkina

ISBN 978-1-8383035-3-2

A Prayer for Family

Dear God,

Thank you for my special family,
for blessing me with love and care.

Thank you for my siblings,
for keeping your arms around them
like a big cuddly bear.

Thank you for my Mommy and Daddy,
for blessing me with the very best.

Thank you Jesus for anointing our family,
at your feet may we always find peace and rest.

Amen

Morning Prayer

Dear God,

Thank you for another day of beautiful sunshine,
and for all the blessings I get to call mine.

Thank you for a good nights rest,
allowing me to be at my very best.

Thank you for my teachers and my school,
for looking out for me, and helping me to keep my cool.

Thank you for your love and protection,
for always helping me and for
giving me good direction.

Amen

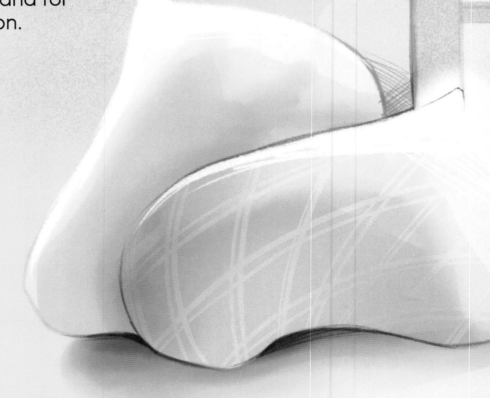

The Lords Armor
Therefore put on the full armor of God, so that when the day of evil comes, you may be able to stand your ground, and after you have done everything, to stand. Stand firm then, with the belt of truth buckled around your waist, with the breastplate of righteousness in place, and with your feet fitted with the readiness that comes from the gospel of peace. In addition to all this, take up the shield of faith, with which you can extinguish all the flaming arrows of the evil one. Take the helmet of salvation and the sword of the Spirit, which is the word of God. **Ephesians 6:13-18**

A Prayer for Help...

Dear God,

Sometimes I get a little bit frustrated,
I know it would be better if I had just waited.

Sometimes I get a little bit mad,
and then afterwards I usually feel sad...

Sometimes I don't know what to say or do,
but luckily for me, I have You.

Please help me Lord to be better,
when I find myself under some pressure.

Amen

Praying for Friends

Dear God,

Thank you for blessing
me with good friends I
can trust,
looking out for each
other is always a must.

Help us all to be
supportive and kind,
always remembering not
to leave anyone behind.

Thank you Lord for these
treasured gems,
help me to see them
through your lens.

Amen

A Prayer for Worry...

Lord you know my heart,
please help it when it gets off to a wobbly start.

There are times when I feel worried about this or that,
or even something small like losing my favorite hat.

Lord you know my thoughts, please help me to keep
them light, like a brightly colored kite.

And when I'm feeling a little uneasy,
grant me your peace to make everything
dandy and breezy.

Amen

Saying Grace

Let us close our eyes and bow our heads,
as we thank God for this delightful spread.

Thank you Lord for our yummy meal,
and for all those that went to a great deal.

We are happy and grateful,
for our delicious plateful.

Amen

Easter Prayer

Today is a special day, to get up and shout hooray!
Jesus has risen, oh today's the day!

Jesus you died on the cross for me and my sin,
as tough as it was, it will forever be my best win.

Thank you for giving me eternal life, love and grace,
forever remembering what you did for me,
for the cross you did embrace.

Amen

A Prayer for Health and Happiness

It's a beautiful day,
to jump up and say...

Thank you Lord for my health,
help me to treasure it like my greatest wealth.

Thank you Lord for all my joy,
allow me to always experience it like I do with my
favorite toy.

Thank you Lord for every smile that comes my way,
let me return the favor and make someone's day.

Thank you Lord for the happiness I feel,
may it be never ending like a giant Ferris wheel!

Amen

Christmas Prayer

Dear God,

On this day, we celebrate your awesome son.
Jesus, The Messiah, the only one.

Thank you Lord for the greatest blessing,
in His hands may I always find a place of resting.

Oh Jesus how we rejoice in this day,
for you entered the world and changed it in
every way.

Amen

A Prayer to Celebrate a New Year!

Oh Lord, it's the start of another year!
I hope and pray it will be one of good cheer.

Help me to be a little more delightful,
to be grateful, helpful and mindful.

Thank you Lord for a fresh new start,
I pray you'll protect and strengthen my heart.

Oh Lord, it's the start of another year!
May I make special memories I'll forever
hold dear.

Amen

Bedtime Prayer

Snuggle up Hunny,
here's a good night kiss from Mommy.

Before you drift off to sleep,
let's say our prayers as God hears our last peep.

Thank you Lord for a fun-filled, joyful day.
Thank you for my family, friends and all I got to play.

Thank you for loving me,
and guiding me throughout each day.

Amen

Additional learning Questions:

- How can we pray to God?
- What is something you want to thank God for today?
- Do you think we need to pray at certain times only?
- Is there anything that you are worried about or scared of that we can speak to God about today?
- What can we pray to God about?
- Is there anyone that needs your prayers today?
- Can you ask Jesus for forgiveness about anything you did or said today?
- Is there something that you can ask God to help you with?

Scripture on prayer:

*And pray in the Spirit on all occasions with all kinds of prayers and requests. With this in mind, be alert and always keep on praying for all the Lord's people. **Ephesians 6:18***

*Then you will call on me and come and pray to me, and I will listen to you. **Jeremiah 28:12***

*Therefore I tell you, whatever you ask for in prayer, believe that you have received it, and it will be yours. **Mark 11:24***

*Rejoice always, pray without ceasing, give thanks in all circumstances, for this is the will of God in Christ Jesus for you. **1 Thessalonians 5:16-18***

Printed in Great Britain
by Amazon